WARNER BROS.
STUDIO TOUR
L O N D O N

THE MAKING OF
Harry Potter ™

THE OFFICIAL GUIDE

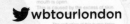 wbtourlondon    wbtourlondon   f facebook.com/wbtourlondon   #WBTourLondon

THE HOME OF HARRY POTTER™

In 2000, an enterprising production team made its way to a film studio on the outskirts of London. The producers brought with them an idea for a film based on a book about a young boy with a lightning bolt scar who, on his eleventh birthday, learns that he is a wizard. That story was *Harry Potter and the Philosopher's Stone™*, and that studio was Leavesden.

Author J.K. Rowling's first four *Harry Potter* books had climbed to top spots on best-seller lists all over the world. The filmmakers, cast and crew were now tasked with bringing to life on the big screen a magical world that was loved by millions.

Hundreds of talented men and women converged at Leavesden Studios to begin more than a decade of production. With each new film, the *Harry Potter* phenomenon grew, and soon the seven books that enchanted the world had become the biggest film series in history.

Warner Bros. Studio Tour London - The Making of Harry Potter™ celebrates the incredible craftsmanship behind these films as well as the wonderful production family that called the Studios home for ten years. The Studio Tour gives fans the unique opportunity to set foot on the actual sets from their favourite movies - at the studios where they were filmed. This Official Guide is the exclusive companion to the Studio Tour. It features a collection of drawings, stories, costumes, photographs and more — all from the series' production here at Warner Bros. Studios Leavesden, the home of *Harry Potter*.

Leavesden functioned as an aircraft factory before becoming a film studio in 1995.

The cast and crew gather for a photo on one of the last days of shooting on *Harry Potter and the Deathly Hallows — Part 2*™.

THE GREAT HALL

As the setting for Hogwarts'™ abundant feasts, the Yule Ball, and even a duel or two, the Great Hall, with its enchanted ceiling, is one of the castle's most unforgettable locations.

The House Points Counter
Though it was rarely seen on screen, prop makers are especially proud of the house points counter, which contains thousands of glass beads.

The Flambeaux
Each of the Great Hall torch holders is a carving of one of the four house animals.

The Owl Lectern
The lectern used by Professor Dumbledore™ is covered in real gold and years of melted wax.

FILM EFFECTS IN THE GREAT HALL
THE ENCHANTED CEILING

The physical ceiling in the Great Hall was inspired by the arched timber ceiling of Westminster Hall in London; however, the Great Hall's enchanted ceiling as seen in the films was created using visual effects.

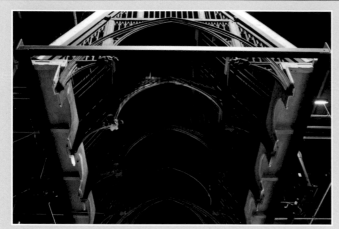

Before
The lighting fixtures and scaffolding in the soundstage were clearly visible above the Great Hall set.

After
The ceiling's wooden beams and swirling clouds were created using computer-generated imagery.

For *Harry Potter and the Philosopher's Stone*, individual candle-shaped tubes containing spirit oil were suspended by wires, which were digitally removed on screen.

Computer-Generated Candles
During production on the first film, the heat from the flames burnt through the wires and the 'candles' fell onto the tables. The floating candles were created digitally thereafter.

6

COSTUMES

Throughout the films, the Costume Designers
gave *Hogwarts* students and staff
their own individual looks and styles.

Gryffindor™   **Ravenclaw™**   **Slytherin™**   **Hufflepuff™**

The *Hogwarts* Staff
From left to right
Professor Moody, Professor Flitwick, Professor Trelawney, Professor McGonagall™, Professor *Dumbledore*,
Professor Snape™, Hagrid™ and Filch.

THE CHOCOLATE FEAST

For the start-of-term feast in Harry Potter and the Goblet of Fire™, the Set Decoration Department created a decadent pudding course.

Sweets and Treats
Chocolate desserts of all kinds covered the Great Hall tables.

Real Chocolate
Several edible desserts were baked, including Swiss rolls and chocolate cakes that cast members were able to eat.

THE YULE BALL

In just over a month, 90 decorators transformed the Great Hall into a ballroom of silvery ice and snow.

Concept sketches for the Yule Ball outfits of Hermione Granger™ and Ron Weasley™.

Yule Ball Costumes

For *Harry Potter and the Goblet of Fire*, Costume Designer Jany Temime created unique gowns and robes for the staff and students, including Harry, Hermione, Viktor Krum™, Cho Chang, and Ron.

GRYFFINDOR™ BOYS' DORMITORY

Up the spiral staircase from the *Gryffindor* common room was the *Gryffindor* boys' dormitory, where Harry and Ron shared a room with Neville Longbottom™, Seamus Finnigan and Dean Thomas.

Harry's New Home
The small, circular shape of the room was Production Designer Stuart Craig's way of creating a space in which Harry would finally feel at home.

Bed Curtains
Designers had originally planned to custom-make the fabric for the curtains surrounding the beds. However, Set Decorator Stephenie McMillan spotted the perfect fabric in a local shop window.

Dormitory Décor
As the boys grew up, the set decorators personalised their spaces in the dormitory; for example, they put up posters and pennants of Ron's favourite Quidditch™ team near his bed.

Originally constructed for *Harry Potter and the Philosopher's Stone*, the beds were much too small for the boys by the later films – and the actors eventually had to curl up to keep their legs and feet from hanging over the ends during shooting.

GRYFFINDOR™ COMMON ROOM

The password 'Caput Draconis' opened the door to the *Gryffindor* common room during Harry, Ron and Hermione's first year at *Hogwarts*.

A Young *Professor McGonagall*
Each portrait on the *Gryffindor* common room walls depicts one of the *Gryffindor* Heads of House, including *Professor McGonagall*.

Wizard's Wireless

The *Gryffindor* common room's radio received news broadcasts from the Wizarding Wireless Network and has an opening on the front grille that actually moves like a talking mouth.

THE DETAILS OF THE COMMON ROOM

The Lady and the Unicorn
The Set Decoration Department chose these tapestries for their medieval look and prominent use of the *Gryffindor* colours — scarlet and gold.

Daniel Radcliffe films his *Triwizard Tournament* first task victory celebration during *Harry Potter and the Goblet of Fire*.

The Invisibility Cloak
Harry Potter's Invisibility Cloak was printed with Celtic symbols and ancient runes. Several cloaks were made, including versions with a green fabric lining that allowed the Visual Effects Department to make Harry and his friends appear to be invisible.

COSTUMES
HARRY, RON AND HERMIONE

Year One
Harry Potter and the Philosopher's Stone

Year Three
Harry Potter and the Prisoner of Azkaban™

Year Seven
Harry Potter and the Deathly Hallows – Part 1™

Hermione, Harry and Ron hide outside Hagrid's hut in *Harry Potter and the Prisoner of Azkaban*

DUMBLEDORE'S OFFICE

Professor Dumbledore's office — a quiet retreat and study for the sage Headmaster — was located in one of the highest towers of *Hogwarts*. Dumbledore's fascination with the universe and the skies became the room's defining feature.

Dumbledore's Bookshelves
Hundreds of books – actually British phonebooks bound in leather – cover the shelves of Dumbledore's study.

During production, the office was adorned with forty-eight portraits of former *Hogwarts* Headmasters.

THE MEMORY CABINET

Dumbledore kept his memories, as well as those he had gathered from other wizards, inside this cabinet which was filled with more than 800 tiny, handmade and hand-labelled vials.

The Sword of *Gryffindor*
The sword itself was purchased, but the hilt was redesigned.

STARGAZING

The Headmaster's shelves glitter with old microscopes, telescopes, star charts and astronomical devices.

Dumbledore's Telescope
Tucked away in the upper chamber was Dumbledore's largest telescope. Though one of the most expensive pieces ever created for the series, it was only ever seen in the background.

COSTUMES
PROFESSOR DUMBLEDORE™

Professor Dumbledore's robes in the first two films appeared medieval in style. They were then given a quirky, 'hippie' touch by Costume Designer Jany Temime from *Harry Potter and the Prisoner of Azkaban* onwards.

Dumbledore's Headmaster Robes: Year One

This costume was worn by Richard Harris in *Harry Potter and the Philosopher's Stone*.

Dumbledore's Headmaster Robes: Year Three

This costume was first worn by Michael Gambon in *Harry Potter and the Prisoner of Azkaban*.

Professor Dumbledore holds an infant *Harry Potter* on Privet Drive in *Harry Potter and the Philosopher's Stone*.

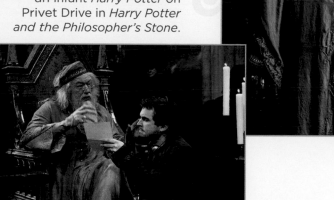

Michael Gambon discusses a scene with Director Alfonso Cuarón during the filming of *Harry Potter and the Prisoner of Azkaban*.

WANDS

More than 3,000 wands were made for the films,
using combinations of wood, plastic, resin and rubber.

Hermione Granger / Ron Weasley / Harry Potter

Lucius Malfoy's staff, which conceals his Wand

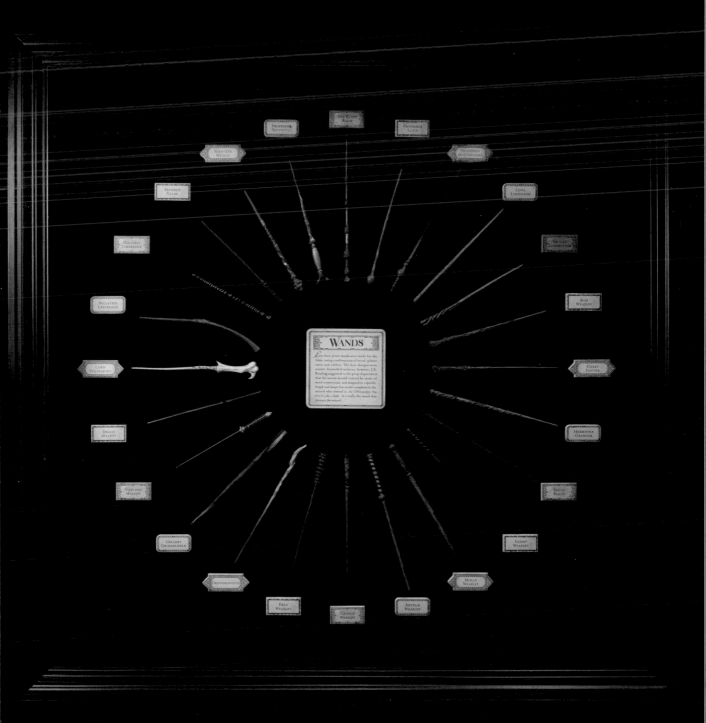

The Wand Chooses the Wizard

J.K. Rowling suggested that each wand should
reflect the personality and characteristics of its owner.
The Prop Making Department's first designs featured ornate
metal scrollwork embedded with precious jewels.
After reviewing these first concepts, Rowling suggested
a much simpler approach instead, using carved materials
like wood and bone.

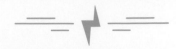

PROP-MAKING MAGIC

A prop is any object, large or small, used by actors or as set decoration on a film. By the time production ended in 2011, the *Harry Potter* Prop Department had filled five giant warehouses with thousands of items (made specially for the films or purchased from a variety of speciality shops), including 5,000 pieces of furniture, 12,000 handmade books and 40,000 Weasleys' Wizard Wheezes products and packages.

The cast films scenes from *Harry Potter and the Goblet of Fire*.

Goblet of Fire™
This final version of the *Goblet of Fire* was hand-carved from the trunk of a single English Elm, and stands over five feet tall.

The Triwizard Cup
This cup, which played a dark role in *Harry Potter and the Goblet of Fire*, is awarded to the winner of the *Triwizard Tournament*. Filmmakers and designers wanted the cup to look like an ever-evolving, organic crystal — as though it had a magical life of its own.

Deluminator
The Prop Department used an old Victorian perfume bottle as Dumbledore's Deluminator.

Time-Turner™
The design team conceived the two proverbs on the *Time-Turner*: *'I mark the hours every one, nor have I yet outrun the sun'* and *'My use and value unto you depends on what you have to do'*.

The Golden Snitch™
Tiny mechanics were handcrafted to allow this *Golden Snitch* to open in *Harry Potter and the Deathly Hallows – Part 2*.

Philosopher's Stone™
During an early conversation with the Art Department, author J.K. Rowling described the *Philosopher's Stone* as 'blood-red', like an uncut ruby.

The Golden Egg
The golden egg that Harry obtained during the first task of the *Triwizard Tournament* is decorated with an etching of an old school building and ancient runes. With one twist of the owl's head on the top, three petals open, revealing the cloudy, bubbly, crystal centre.

Remembrall™
During his first year, *Neville Longbottom* received this *Remembrall* from his grandmother. The orb fills with red smoke when the holder has forgotten something.

THE HORCRUXES

In an attempt to achieve immortality, Lord Voldemort™ concealed fragments of his soul in Horcruxes—one of which was his snake, Nagini. Prop makers created detailed versions of the other Horcruxes for close-ups, stunt work and special effects shots.

Rowena Ravenclaw's Diadem

Helga Hufflepuff's Cup

Tom Riddle's™ Diary

Marvolo Gaunt's Ring

Harry Potter™

Unbeknownst to *Lord Voldemort*, another final horcrux was embedded in *Harry Potter* himself during the confrontation that gave the boy wizard his lightning bolt scar when he was only one year old.

Salazar Slytherin's Locket

THE ANIMALS OF THE WIZARDING WORLD

The soundstages and backlot of Leavesden were home to a veritable zoo of animals, all cared for by the Animal Department. The decade-long production schedule of the films gave the animal trainers the unique opportunity to watch their animal actors grow, mature and learn many new tricks.

Hedwig™

Hedwig was played by four different bright and beautiful snowy owls – each one trained to perform very specific actions.

Scabbers™

More than a dozen different rats played Ron's pet, *Scabbers*, and the Creature Effects Department even developed an animatronic double.

Harry and *Hedwig* sit in the *Gryffindor* common room.

Ron practises spells on *Scabbers* during Transfiguration lessons.

Fang

The Animal Department cast a team of nine Neapolitan Mastiffs to play *Hagrid's* dog Fang, the cause of a *lot* of slobber on set!

Crookshanks™

Four talented Red Persian cats played Hermione's cat, *Crookshanks*. To make these beautiful pets appear a little more unkempt, the Animal Department attached matted fur to them using hair clips.

'Monkey', one of the animal actors that played Fang, prepares for his daily walk.

Hagrid (Robbie Coltrane) appears with one of the Fang actors.

Emma Watson poses for a photo with *Crookshanks* on the set of *Harry Potter and the Prisoner of Azkaban*.

POTIONS

Potions class was taught by *Professor Snape*, and later Professor Slughorn, in a dark classroom lined with dusty shelves full of peculiar jars and bottles.

The Classroom
The Art Department designed this room to appear as though it were located in a dark, underground corner of the castle.

Ginger Root & Salamanders
Among the ingredients kept on the classroom shelves were baked animal bones from a local butcher shop, dried leaves and herbs, and other objects.

Gilded Archways
These brass-leafed archways are inscribed with the
Latin and English names of potion ingredients and rare
minerals, all selected from ancient alchemy recipes.

HAGRID'S HUT

This is the home of Rubeus Hagrid™, Keeper of Keys and Grounds at *Hogwarts* and, later, Care of Magical Creatures teacher.

Hut Renovations
In *Harry Potter and the Prisoner of Azkaban*, *Hagrid's* hut expanded to include a pumpkin patch and a second room.

A Half-Giant Costume
This costume from *Harry Potter and the Order of the Phoenix™* fits the frame of a 6'10" double for *Hagrid* (though *Hagrid* is described in the fiction as being much taller).

Special Effects
Filmmakers relied on some clever tricks to make *Hagrid* seem larger than the other characters, including creating two different versions of the set. A larger scale set was used to make characters of 'regular' size seem small in comparison to the surroundings, and a smaller set was used to make *Hagrid* (Robbie Coltrane) seem large.

Inside the Hut
Set decorators filled the hut with an abundance of cages, each containing peculiar animals and items such as hairless cats, fruit bats, and ostrich eggs.

QUIDDITCH™

In the wizarding sport of *Quidditch*, two teams — each made up of three Chasers, two Beaters, one Keeper and one Seeker — zoom around an open field on broomsticks trying to send a ball known as a 'Quaffle' through the opposing team's hoops and catch the *Golden Snitch*. With this basic rulebook in mind, filmmakers developed *Quidditch* into a real sport that they could capture on film.

Daniel Radcliffe and Tom Felton film a *Quidditch* match for Harry Potter and the Chamber of Secrets™.

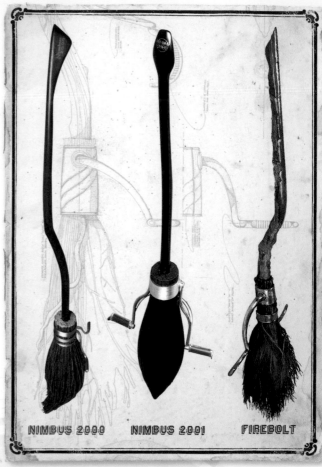

NIMBUS 2000   NIMBUS 2001   FIREBOLT

BROOMSTICKS

Each of the flying broomsticks was individually designed by the Art Department and brought to life by the Prop Making Department. Brooms were manufactured to be light enough for an owl or an eleven-year-old Harry to carry easily while others had to be rugged enough to support an actor whilst spinning, dipping and diving during an effects rig.

Quidditch Equipment
The Art Department designed a full set of official *Quidditch* equipment, the Prop Department then made that equipment based on those designs, costumers created *Quidditch* uniforms, and graphic designers developed pennants and posters for supporters to show their house pride.

Golden Snitch™
After several versions, including some with insect wings, filmmakers settled on this *Golden Snitch*, which was actually gold-plated.

FILM EFFECTS

From flying motorbikes to fire-breathing dragons, everything magical in the *Harry Potter* films required the real-world wizardry of special and visual effects.

SPECIAL EFFECTS

The Special Effects Department oversees all of the hands-on, physical effects that operate in front of the camera, including everything from motorised gadgets to real explosions.

Hungarian Horntail
The Special Effects Department developed flamethrowers for the Hungarian Horntail that shot fireballs more than 12 metres.

VISUAL EFFECTS

The Visual Effects Department designs the computer-generated characters, environments and enhancements that the camera is unable to capture.

Centaurs
The Visual Effects Department created a computer-generated centaur for *Harry Potter and the Philosopher's Stone*.

THE MAGIC OF GREENSCREEN

Filmmakers often shoot visual effects scenes on a green screen, which allows them to replace the green colours with a completely different background or computer-generated set.

Emma Watson and Daniel Radcliffe film in front of a green screen during *Harry Potter and the Deathly Hallows — Part 1*.

 Colours and Contrast
Chroma green is the colour most often used in filming visual effects, though it's not uncommon to use *chroma blue* or *chroma violet* when a character or costume is coloured green.

The Griffin Stairwell

Two versions of the beautifully sculpted stairs leading to Dumbledore's office were created, including a static model and a second, fully-functioning version that required some incredibly complex mechanics.

Chamber of Secrets™ Door

Many fans assume that the *Chamber of Secrets* door was a computer-generated effect. In fact, this intricate device was hand built by the Special Effects Department.

Daniel Radcliffe films on the Griffin Stairwell set.

Harry approaches the door to the *Chamber of Secrets*.

Hagrid's Motorbike

The Special Effects Department customised seven versions of this 1960 Royal Enfield motorbike, each modified with a larger seat to fit the half-giant *Hagrid*.

Robbie Coltrane and Daniel Radcliffe shoot the 'Seven Harrys' sequence of *Harry Potter and the Deathly Hallows — Part 1.*

THE BURROW

On his first visit to The Burrow in *Harry Potter and the Chamber of Secrets*, Harry marvelled at the Weasleys' collection of wonderful, magical curiosities.

The Weasley Home
The Burrow was designed to look as though Mr Weasley had built it all—including a pigsty.

Magical Effects
The Special Effects Department created several magical household items that physically operated on camera, like the self-washing frying pan.

Shooting an exterior scene of The Burrow for Harry Potter and the Half-Blood Prince™.

The Weasley Family Clock
This rather unique clock was purchased at a local auction. Prop makers outfitted it with new pendulums, gears, hands and other fanciful accessories to turn it into the clock that let Mrs Weasley know where each member of her family was at all times.

Building The Burrow

No wall in The Burrow was at a right angle, with every surface deliberately sloped. To achieve this off-kilter look, the talented construction crew pushed and pulled support beams and wall units out of place with chains after the set was constructed (whilst keeping the set structurally sound).

MEETING AT MALFOY™ MANOR

Lord Voldemort gathered the *Death Eaters* here in *Malfoy* Manor
to plan the takeover of the Ministry of Magic.
Malfoy Manor, Draco's ominous childhood home, was designed
in stark contrast to Harry's modest upbringing in the cupboard
under the stairs at number four, Privet Drive.

Charity Burbage

The Creature Effects Department
created a full-sized, writhing animatronic of Charity
Burbage to stand-in for actress Carolyn Pickles in
long shots. For close-ups, Ms. Pickles was harnessed
and suspended upside-down above the table.

The Riddle Family Gravestone

The inspiration for this gravestone came from Highgate
Cemetery in North London, though artists altered its angelic
design by using the 'Angel of Death'.

Nagini

Nagini the snake was captured on film in several variations. During production, Nagini was played by a real snake as well as several, full-size replicas handcrafted by the Creature Effects Department. The final scenes were augmented with a digital version of Nagini created by the Visual Effects Department.

THE MINISTRY OF MAGIC

Concealed deep beneath the streets of London,
the Wizarding World's centre of government in Britain is
accessible by telephone booth, toilet and the Floo Network.

The Towers

The office towers were based on a 19th century
Victorian building in London and covered with
thousands of green and red tiles made of wood.

Extras at the Ministry

As the Ministry of Magic was
one of the largest sets ever
constructed for the films, scenes
shot there required hundreds
of extras—many of whom were
actually crewmembers in cloaks,
beards and hats.

The Fireplaces
Each of the Ministry's enormous fireplaces was over nine metres tall.

Magic is Might
The statue — including the fifty-eight Muggles™ at the base being crushed under the rule of the Wizarding World — was sculpted from foam and hand-painted.

UMBRIDGE'S MINISTRY OF MAGIC OFFICE

Dolores Umbridge's Ministry of Magic office retains many of the nuances that were featured in her office at *Hogwarts* —especially the gaudy pink motif.

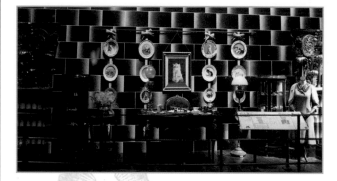

Office Furnishings
Professor Umbridge had a love of ornate furniture, which set decorators found at a Middle Eastern furniture shop tucked away in North London.

The Kitten Plates
From white kittens to peculiar-looking hairless breeds, dozens of cats were filmed with goldfish bowls, crystal balls, miniature witches' hats and other props. The Visual Effects Department digitally added the frisky feline footage to the plates during post-production.

On the set, each of the kitten plates in Umbridge's *Hogwarts* office had a bluescreen centre that was replaced during post-production.

COSTUMES
PROFESSOR UMBRIDGE™

Shades of Pink
As she gained more and more power at the Ministry of Magic, Dolores Umbridge's wardrobe became progressively pinker.

Imelda Staunton discusses a scene with director David Yates while filming *Harry Potter and the Order of the Phoenix*.

THE DARK ARTS

The Dark Arts, also known as Dark Magic, refers to magic that is mainly used to control or cause harm and even death to a victim.

Though Dark Arts aren't necessarily "evil", the practice is discouraged. Some Dark Arts artefacts (like the Vanishing Cabinet and The Hand of Glory) were created early in the film series, when the producers were still unaware of J.K. Rowling's plans to include them in the plot twists still to come in the later motion pictures.

To construct the skull-like Death Eater masks, the Creature Effects Department made life casts of each actor's face. The moulds were then used by the Prop Department to create the unique masks with a weathered pewter finish.

Giant Spiders
To bring Aragog to life, the Creature Effects Department built a huge, physical animatronic that spanned 18 feet (5.5 metres) across. Aragog was filmed creeping out of the tree roots, which hid the wiring, mechanics and support crew.

Towering Trees
The trees of the Forbidden Forest were built to a massive scale, reaching diameters of 12 to 14 feet (4.3 metres).

THE FORBIDDEN FOREST

The Dark Forest (as it was originally known) has appeared in one form or another in every *Harry Potter* film. Early on, the scenes were shot on location at Black Park in Buckinghamshire, but shooting in a real forest, where the environment couldn't be controlled, proved difficult. As the series progressed, the production team decided to build sets for the forest instead.

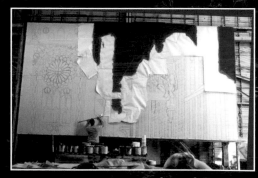

Painted Forests
The hand-painted backdrops were up to 600 feet (183 metres) wide and among some of the largest ever created.

PLATFORM 9¾™ & HOGWARTS EXPRESS™

The *Hogwarts Express* locomotive transported hundreds of students from *Platform 9¾* to *Hogwarts School of Witchcraft and Wizardry*. Most of the scenes that take place on *Platform 9¾* were actually shot on location at King's Cross Station in London, however, during *Harry Potter and the Deathly Hallows – Part 2*, part of the station platform was recreated on a soundstage here at Leavesden, complete with the track and the train.

FIRST SHOT & LAST SHOT

The *Hogwarts Express* provided the background for the very first shot ever captured for *Harry Potter and the Philosopher's Stone*, and then, ten years later, for the very last shot of the entire series in *Harry Potter and the Deathly Hallows – Part 2*.

INTERIOR CARRIAGES

The real locomotive and passenger carriages were used on locations throughout the United Kingdom to create the exterior views of the train while a special interior carriage set (built in front of a green or blue screen on the soundstages at Leavesden) was used for all of the scenes that take place inside the train. Visual effects artists replaced the green and blue in the windows with moving backdrops and special effects like hopping Chocolate Frogs and flying Dementors™.

THE HOGWARTS EXPRESS™

Before the bright red *Hogwarts Express* became one of the most iconic vehicles in motion picture history, it served as a working passenger locomotive from April of 1937 until its retirement in December of 1963. The train consists of a GWR 4900 Class 5972 Olton Hall locomotive and tender pulling British Rail Mark 1 carriages. This was the first passenger carriage designed to work across all the different rail lines in England following the nationalisation of the railways in 1957.

GRAPHICS DEPARTMENT

Schoolbooks and versions of the Marauder's Maps, *Quidditch* programme and wanted posters, *Honeydukes* sweets and Wizarding Wheezes; all of these printed pieces were generated by the Graphics Department.

PRODUCT LABELS

This small team of artists (led by Miraphora Mina and Eduardo Lima) created every page, poster, package, proclamation and paper, including hundreds of copies of *The Quibbler* and the *Daily Prophet*.

Wanted Posters

Quidditch™ Programme

THE QUIBBLER™ AND THE DAILY PROPHET™

The Graphics Department designed and printed over forty editions of
the *Daily Prophet* and more than 25,000 pages of *The Quibbler*. Each page
featured unique stories, headlines, advertisements and even horoscopes.
To everyone's amusement, the team often included references to members
of the cast and crew in the newspaper content.

THE MARAUDER'S MAP

The Marauder's Map was designed by the Graphics Department, using
lines made of handwritten text that included names and hidden messages.
After first appearing in *Harry Potter and the Prisoner of Azkaban*,
the Marauder's Map was redesigned for each subsequent film with
new layers, hallways and calligraphy.

THE BACKLOT

During production, the backlot was home to the exterior sets of the *Harry Potter* films—including Privet Drive and the *Hogwarts* bridge.

The Ford Anglia
In total, 16 Ford Anglias* were created for *Harry Potter and the Chamber of Secrets*, including one that was cut in half for filming.

Rupert Grint and Daniel Radcliffe film the Ford Anglia* flight sequence for *Harry Potter and the Chamber of Secrets*.

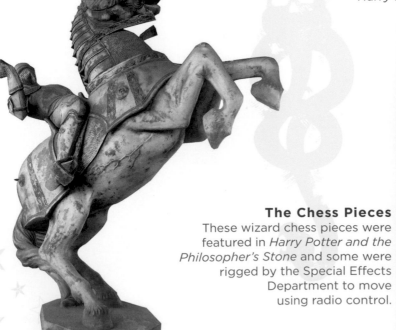

The Chess Pieces
These wizard chess pieces were featured in *Harry Potter and the Philosopher's Stone* and some were rigged by the Special Effects Department to move using radio control.

On the Backlot
The Studio Tour backlot features a number
of exterior sets, sculptures and vehicles,
which were often used in scenes that were
filmed on-location, away from the Studios.

THE BACKLOT
KNIGHT BUS™

The 22-foot tall *Knight Bus* was created from pieces of three vintage London double-deckers.

Interior shots of the *Knight Bus* were filmed on a soundstage.

Building the Knight Bus™
Two versions of the bus were built: one that was motorised and able to be driven and a 'stunt' version that spun around on a turntable.

PRIVET DRIVE

Number four, Privet Drive was the quiet, suburban home of the Dursleys, the relatives who raised *Harry Potter* after his parents' unexpected deaths.

The 'Seven Harrys' scene from *Harry Potter and the Deathly Hallows — Part 1*, was filmed on the Leavesden Backlot.

Filming at Privet Drive
The exterior of the house in *Harry Potter and the Philosopher's Stone* was filmed in Bracknell, Berkshire. For future films, the filmmakers decided to recreate the street on the backlot.

THE BACKLOT
HOGWARTS™ BRIDGE

Though it was never in the original novel or script, the now iconic Hogwarts bridge was created for *Harry Potter and the Prisoner of Azkaban*.

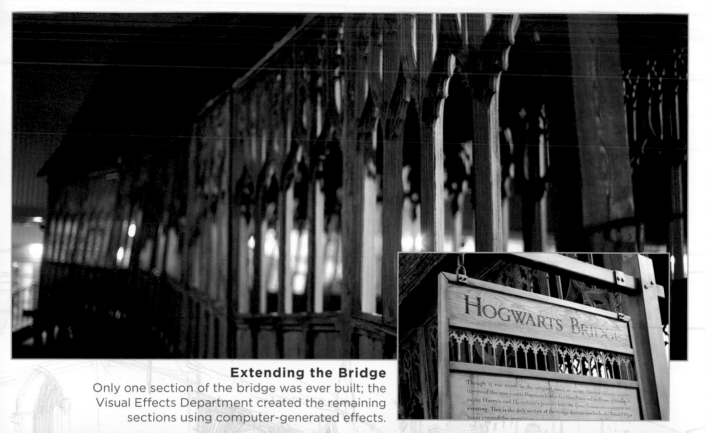

Extending the Bridge
Only one section of the bridge was ever built; the Visual Effects Department created the remaining sections using computer-generated effects.

Emma Watson and Daniel Radcliffe film a scene on the *Hogwarts* bridge during *Harry Potter and the Goblet of Fire*.

CREATURE EFFECTS

The *Harry Potter* films called for hundreds of creatures and intricate prosthetics—from the Basilisk and Buckbeak™ to *Lord Voldemort's* snake-like face—all built by Creature Effects.

Makeup and Mandrakes
Creature Effects created the makeup effects for characters like Griphook the goblin, and built other creatures, like the Mandrakes, using animatronics made of steel and foam.

A *Gringotts* goblin features in a scene from *Harry Potter and the Philosopher's Stone.*

Creature Models
Creature Effects also created models called maquettes, which were scanned by the Visual Effects Department who then developed their own computer-generated versions.

Hungarian Horntail

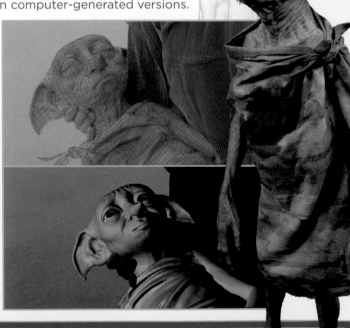

Dobby The House-Elf
Creature Effects built a life-size version of *Dobby* for the actors to work with in *Harry Potter and the Deathly Hallows—Part 1.* The Visual Effects Department then scanned that version into the computer, and applied computer-generated facial expressions and movement to create the *Dobby* seen on screen.

Creature Creation
Creature Effects was filled with everything from motors, gears and remote controls to paint, plaster moulds and rubber masks.

THE CREATURES

ARAGOG

Aragog had an 18-foot leg span and was covered by hand with yak hair, sisal (a fibrous plant of the agave family) and hemp from brooms. The animatronic figure was so complex that it required nearly 100 technicians to operate.

BUCKBEAK™

Three life-size, animatronic versions of *Buckbeak* were built: one standing, another rearing and a third lying down. Visual effects artists also scanned a life-size version of *Buckbeak* to create a digital model, which was then animated for *Harry Potter and the Prisoner of Azkaban*.

FAWKES™

Three animatronic versions of *Fawkes* were built: an old, moulting phoenix, a new-born bird that rises from the ashes and a (non-moulting) adult phoenix. A computer-generated version of *Fawkes* was also made from digitally scanned models of the bird.

MAKEUP AND PROSTHETICS

GREYBACK

Makeup effects artists in Creature Effects developed a seven-piece silicone prosthetic mask for Greyback's werewolf face.

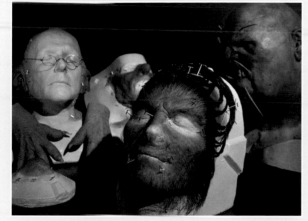

Werewolf Fur
Each prosthetic was made with real goat hair that was inserted strand-by-strand.

Makeup artists apply werewolf makeup and prosthetics to Dave Legeno during *Harry Potter and the Deathly Hallows — Part 1*.

VOLDEMORT™

The makeup effects used to create the Dark Lord included temporary tattoos for veins, enhanced cheekbones, contact lenses, and false eyebrows, fingernails and teeth.

Visual Effects
Coloured dots on actor Ralph Fiennes's face were used to track the movement of his face and digitally replace his nose with Voldemort's snake-like nostrils.

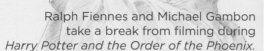

Ralph Fiennes and Michael Gambon take a break from filming during *Harry Potter and the Order of the Phoenix*.

GRINGOTTS™ WIZARDING BANK

BANKING HALL COLUMNS
The illusion of *Gringotts'* majestic marble columns required layers of painstaking construction and paint effects to create.

BANKING HALL FLOORS
The highly detailed and polished floors of the *Gringotts* banking hall as seen in *Deathly Hallows - Part 2* were actually made of paper. To achieve the look of a marble floor, a visual design was first created in the Art Department.

CHANDELIER DESIGN

Several massive chandeliers were constructed for the *Gringotts* Wizarding Bank set — each strung with thousands of plastic 'crystals'. While Production Designer Stuart Craig's chandelier design measured twelve feet wide and sixteen feet from top to bottom, to reduce production costs, only the lower halves of the chandeliers were created physically, while the top halves seen on screen were added as a computer-generated effect.

During the *Gringotts* break-in scene in *Deathly Hallows - Part 2*, Hermione transforms into Bellatrix Lestrange using a Polyjuice Potion in order to gain access to her family vault.

THE GRINGOTTS™ VAULTS

Harry discovered the depths of *Gringotts* during his first ride in this *Gringotts* vault cart in *Harry Potter and the Philosopher's Stone*. A decade later, the vault cart would be restyled to accommodate the exciting chase scenes of *Deathly Hallows - Part 2*. These gave the vault cart more screen time, requiring a heartier design and the ability to whip along a serpentine track.

Like so many scenes in the films, the *Gringotts* vault sequence seen in *Harry Potter and the Deathly Hallows–Part 2* was a combination of both special effects and visual effects.

THE VAULT CART SEQUENCE

Construction
The vault cart was built by the Special Effects Department, and then mechanised with motors that enabled it to move up, down and around in six different directions.

Filming
The vault cart was attached to a state-of-the-art motion rig, which also provided the movement for broomsticks, *Hagrid's* motorbike and the *Gringotts* dragon's back.

Post-Production
Digital artists built a 3D computer-generated version of the underground *Gringotts* set based on illustrations, which was combined with the green screen footage.

LESTRANGE VAULT

Thousands of pieces of fake treasure were created to fill the Lestrange vault, including the *Hufflepuff* cup, *Death Eater* masks, and skeletons. A machine in the studio ran non-stop for three months just to produce all the cups needed for the treasure replication scene alone. Because those multiplying cups needed to fully surround and cover the actors in the scene, they were made with a special soft foam to prevent injury.

Overall, 38,000 pieces of rubberised treasure were used in the Lestrange vault scene, including 7,014 Hufflepuff cups — only four of which were made of copper and gold plated for use in close-ups.

THE DRAGON ESCAPE SEQUENCE

Construction
The small portion of the dragon's back with which the actors interacted was built by the Creature Effects and Special Effects Departments.

Filming
Actors and stunt doubles were filmed on a green screen soundstage, giving the Visual Effects team complete control over the sequence.

Post-Production
After filming, digital artists combined this section of the dragon's back with a fully computer-generated creature to create the final film scene.

The Production of Destruction
To shoot a scene of destruction, filmmakers couldn't just wreck an existing set; they had to build a new one. Designing that destroyed set required a careful combination of storytelling, research, and art. Stuart Craig and his team turned to the architectural drawings of the *Gringotts* banking hall from the first film to determine a logical arrangement for how the same room might appear when destroyed by a dragon in *Deathly Hallows - Part 2*.

Harry, Ron and Hermione escape from *Gringotts* bank on the back of the dragon.

DIAGON ALLEY™

The *Diagon Alley* set constantly changed throughout the film series. Since its construction, walls have shifted, shop fronts have moved and entire buildings have been carefully tweaked, leaning just slightly, to create the street that is seen in the films.

Building a Village
Many of the *Diagon Alley* set pieces were re-dressed for use in the village of Hogsmeade™ for *Harry Potter and the Prisoner of Azkaban*.

Quirky Shoppers
Each of the shopkeepers and patrons was
given his or her own unique costume.

Designing Diagon Alley™
The original design of the street combined the
rich details from the *Harry Potter* books with
inspiration from the streets described in the
works of Charles Dickens.

DIAGON ALLEY™ : THE SHOPS
WEASLEYS' WIZARD WHEEZES

In this three-storey explosion of orange in a deserted *Diagon Alley*, the Weasley twins sold everything from Extendable Ears to fireworks.

The Weasleys' Wares
The 120 individually designed products reflected Fred and George's mischievous sense of humour.

The cast and crew film a scene from *Harry Potter and the Half-Blood Prince* inside the Weasleys' Wizard Wheezes set.

Building the Joke Shop
Designed to look like an 18th century shop, the Weasleys' storefront took more than three months to build—and much of that time was spent constructing the 20-foot mannequin above the main entrance.

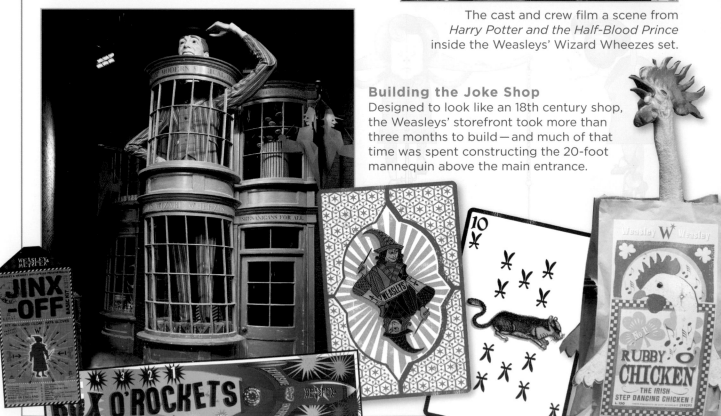

DIAGON ALLEY™:
THE SHOPS
GRINGOTTS™ BANK

In its labyrinth of underground vaults, goblin-run *Gringotts* is the safest place in the Wizarding World to store anything valuable.

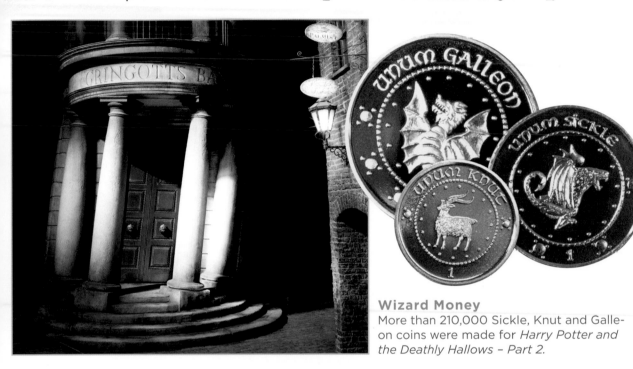

Wizard Money
More than 210,000 Sickle, Knut and Galleon coins were made for *Harry Potter and the Deathly Hallows – Part 2*.

OLLIVANDERS™ WAND SHOP

This dusty shop in *Diagon Alley* with its tightly packed shelves is where Harry's wand chose him.

Wand Boxes
Ollivanders was home to more than 17,000 individually labelled wand boxes.

Harry tries out a wand given to him by Mr Ollivander (John Hurt) in *Harry Potter and the Philosopher's Stone*.

HOGWARTS™ CASTLE MODEL

This is a jewel in the crown of the Art Department:
the intricately detailed model of *Hogwarts* castle.
Built for the first film, *Harry Potter and the Philosopher's Stone*,
the model's every courtyard, tower and turret were filmed and
enhanced with digital effects to create unforgettably realistic
views of the magical school.

The Castle Grounds
Footage of this meticulously built model
was combined with digital effects to create
unforgettably realistic views of the exterior of
Hogwarts School of Witchcraft and Wizardry.

From Sketch to Set
Model makers built this 1:24 scale model based on
Production Designer Stuart Craig's initial concept sketch.

CONSTRUCTION

A team of 86 artists and crew members built the first version of *Hogwarts* castle *for Harry Potter and the Philosopher's Stone*.

REAL CASTLES

To make *Hogwarts* appear even more realistic, artists built miniature versions of courtyards and towers inspired by Alnwick Castle and Durham Cathedral, where scenes from *Harry Potter and the Philosopher's Stone* were shot.

LAKES & HILLSIDES

The *Hogwarts* landscape is inspired by the Highlands of Scotland, including the regions of Glen Nevis, Glen Coe and Loch Shiel.

SECRETS OF THE MODEL

LIGHTS & TORCHES

Model makers installed more than 300 fibre optic lights, which simulate lanterns and torches and even gave the illusion of students passing through the hallways.

TINY DETAILS

Everything is perfectly hand-sculpted to scale.

TREES & BOULDERS

Artists used real gravel for rockwork and boulders, and real plants for landscaping and trees.

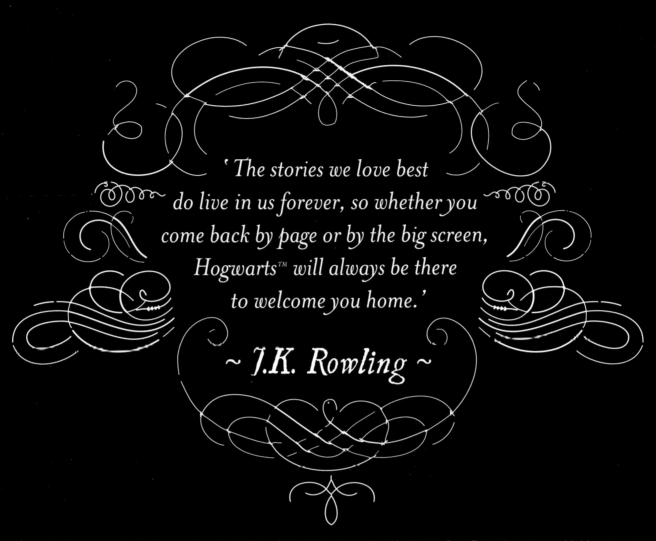

' *The stories we love best*
do live in us forever, so whether you
come back by page or by the big screen,
Hogwarts™ will always be there
to welcome you home.'

~ J.K. Rowling ~

Warner Bros. Studio Tour London - The Making of Harry Potter is produced by Warner Bros. Entertainment, a worldwide leader in the production and distribution of feature films, television programming, home entertainment, comic books, product and brand licensing, games, and interactive entertainment.

To learn more about Warner Bros. Studio Tour London - The Making of Harry Potter, please visit **www.wbstudiotour.co.uk**, and for Warner Bros. Entertainment, please visit **www.warnerbros.com**.

Acknowledgements: The Blair Partnership, Mark Hutchinson Management, StonehillSalt PR, Thinkwell Group, E. Morrison, and the filmmakers, cast and crew of the Harry Potter films.

Cover design by MinaLima.

Warner Bros. Studio Tour London would like to extend a special thank you to author J.K. Rowling for her guidance and support.

WIZARDING
WORLD

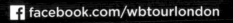